INTRODUCTION

Millions of years ago the Cheshire Plain was submerged by the sea. Later, Iron Age Britons, who built forts on wooded ridges, were followed by the Romans who made the walled city of Chester a major stronghold to protect the surrounding area from Welsh tribesmen and marauders. The River Dee now runs gently through rich farmland past this city with its well preserved Roman remains and medieval architecture, then across a vast sandy estuary out to the Irish Sea. Today, cattle graze lazily on the green slopes; there are woodlands and meres and typical black and white 'magpie' houses among rhododendrons. On the hilltops, there are traces of ramparts and spectacular views, especially near Tarporley, where eight counties can be seen. To the south near the Welsh border, set in rich farmland with houses and half-timbered cottages.

To the north, the land sweeps across to the River Mersey, where seaside resorts lie near to the industrial scene of Ellesmere Port with its cranes and oil-refinery tanks. Across the border is the North Wales coalfield, the centre of which is Mold, the county town of Clwyd. Four miles south west of the town is Llanferres in the foothills of the Clwydian Range: a good vantage point for viewing the surrounding countryside. Below is the Vale of Llangollen, where some of the most spectacular scenery in Wales can be seen.

Mountain ranges overlook lush green valleys and woodland scenery. There are fine walks and burial sites and ancient monuments to be explored.

CONTENTS

Llangollen near the River Dee (Ref: 2142. Picture: D. Pratt)

The Eastgate Clock Tower at Chester (Picture: D. Pratt)

© Alan Kind 1990. All rights reserved. No part of this publication may be reproduced without the prior permission of David & Charles plc. Typeset by Typesetters (Birmingham) Ltd, Smethwick, West Midlands and printed in Great Britain by Redwood Press Ltd, Melksham, Wiltshire for David & Charles plc Brunel House Newton Abbot Devon

Any spot on a Landranger 1/50,000 map can be located by use of a National Grid reference. This is done by noting which vertical line falls to the left of the location and then which horizontal line falls below the location. For example, if we had arranged to meet a friend at the Iron Age hill fort at Bickerton this falls within the one kilometre square labelled 490520.

We next estimate tenths of a square to the right of the vertical grid line, and tenths of a square above the horizontal grid line, to give a standard six figure grid reference which, in this case, is 497529. You may find it helpful to imagine nine vertical lines and nine horizontal lines in each small square when doing this. On the ground these imaginary lines represent squares of one hundred metres edge (about a hundred and ten old fashioned yards).

Some important guide books, such as those of the National Trust and the Ramblers Association, now use map references and from these the exact location of anything from a stately home to a farmhouse offering bed and breakfast can be identified.

Here is another example. If we wish to refer to the triangulation pillar in kilometre square 250500 then, by estimating tenths of a square, we get the full six-figure reference 257509.

This is all that is needed by way of referencing on a single Landranger map although, by adding letters to a reference, one can specify anywhere in Britain, on any modern Ordnance Survey (OS)

map, of any scale. If you are interested in doing this, look at the instructions in the margin of the map.

Here is a useful hint for reading and measuring OS map references: "across the plain and up the hill". This will remind you to run your eye horizontally from left to right to get the "Eastings" before you run your eye from bottom to top to get the "Northings". Remember that the hint tells you which way you must run your eyes NOT which way the grid lines run!

Right, what is the six figure OS reference for the Youth Hostel at Tyndwr Hall which is in the bottom left hand corner of the map? Next what feature is located by 332772? If you get these two OS references right you can get any OS reference right.

(Answers: The Youth Hostel at Tyndwr Hall is at 231413. The OS reference 332772 gives the position of the picnic site at Willaston).

Reading a map reference

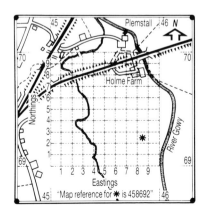

The Chester and Wrexham area is steeped in history, much of which still survives today. A number of Roman roads radiate from Chester, but more famous is the magnificent Offa's Dyke Path, which passes through some of the most breath-taking scenery in the area. Another earthwork, Wat's Dyke, can also be walked along, but this is much smaller than Offa's masterpiece.

The area is a popular tourist spot, understandably, and in response to this a number of footpaths have been developed, of which the Sandstone Trail is probably the best, although all are good.

Roman Roads: Chester was one of the main legionary fortresses on the Welsh borders, and an important base for military operations against Wales. Thus the city needed to be well supplied, and Roman roads can still be seen in the area.

The most important of the supply roads to Chester was Watling Street (West). Watling Street was the main arterial highway from the Channel ports of Kent, north-west across the country to Wroxeter. But another important Roman road known as Watling Street branched off from Wroxeter in a south to north direction. This was the main road for military operations in this turbulent area, and for the purposes of clarity is known as Watling Street (West).

The road left Chester and crossed the River Dee at a point very close to the modern bridge (407658), and followed the line of

the modern road to Eccleston, and then ran as a track to Eaton Hall (417608).

Excavations of the Roman road between Chester and Eaton Hall have found some interesting and relatively sophisticated construction methods. At Stonehouse near Chester the road was covered with stone flags $18 \times 12 \times 8$ inches thick. But another excavation near Heronbridge (410640) discovered a more elaborate construction. Margary described it as "a layer of cobbles, two deep, with a layer of gravel 10–15 inches thick above, between two stone kerbs, the extreme width including these being 30 feet 9 inches." On the east side of this was another metalled layer, of sandstone with cobbles . . . "perhaps an earlier surface".

The route crossed the River Dee again to the north of Aldford church (417601), and it is marked today by a track to the motte and

A railway walk in The Wirral

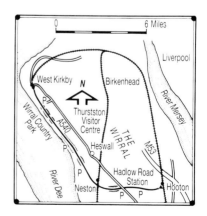

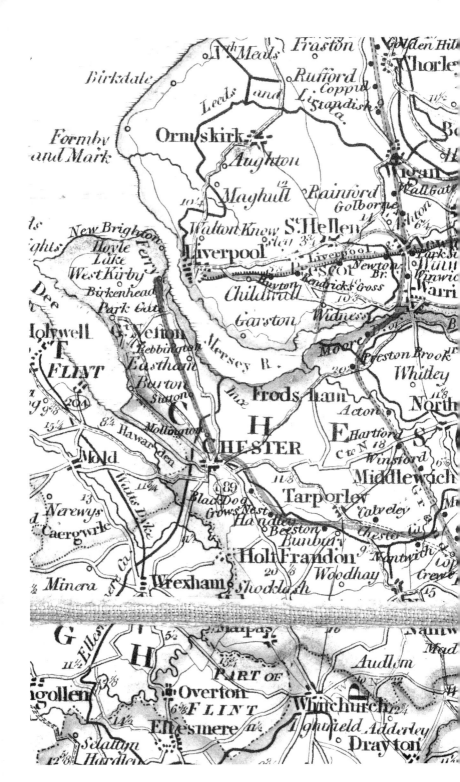

Part of J. Wyld's map of Britain, 1843 (enlarged)

6

bailey castle. A change of alignment was made on the high ground near the church to south-south-east, and this is clearly visible as a green lane with an agger twenty-four feet wide and a foot high (424570).

Unfortunately, the alignment is unclear between Churton and Tilston (460513), but from Tilston the alignment is followed quite closely by the modern B5395 for five miles through Malpas. At the Hough (496462) the Roman road continues straight on as a track to Grindley Brook, and this is where all firm evidence of the route runs out.

Another important Roman road leaving Chester leads to Manchester, before turning to the northern frontier. Today it is rep-resented by the A51(T) as far as Stamford Bridge, and then as a footpath to Street Farm (500680). The alignment of the road is typically Roman and beautifully straight.

On Kelsall Hill the road is very clear, first as a hollow way, but then as a large agger forty feet wide (540688). This continues to Eddisbury Hill, and finally the road exits the area in fine style in the form of the A556(T) (600704).

Relatively recently, another Roman road leading from Chester was found heading in a north-westerly direction to the Wirral peninsula. Initially its course is unknown, but it is thought that the A540 represents it quite accurately as far as Crabwall Hall (387696).

The departure of the Romans welcomed in an age of Celtic cul-

Part of David & Charles 1st Edition OS Map, Sheet No 26

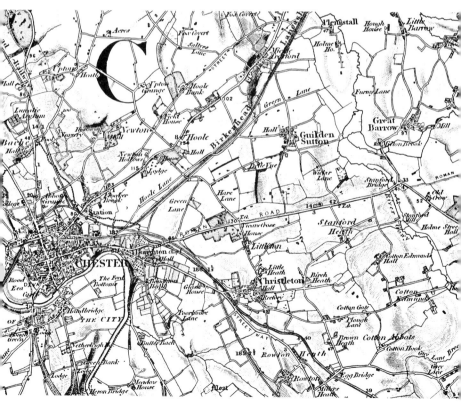

ture. Aethelfrith's victory at Chester marked the beginning of a definite Welsh nation, for Aethelfrith of Northumbria had the leadership of the English, but Mercia and Wessex retained their independence with pride. By pushing forward the frontiers of the Mercian Kingdom as far as Oswestry, Penda, the King of Mercia, prepared the way for the famed Offa.

It was Offa who built the great Dyke, which today forms the basis of one of Britain's finest long distance paths. The Dyke itself is somewhat of a contradiction, almost a propaganda exercise. It was built to keep any possible aggressors out, but its sheer size and presence represents more of a statement of power than a territorial boundary.

The first section of the path in the area is across a block of moorland between Llandegla and Llangollen (210420). The path here is some way away from the dyke itself, which runs through what is now a more populated stretch between Tanyfron (293521), Coedpoeth (294514) and Ruabon (300447).

The path has been designed to keep more to the wild countryside, to give a feeling of what travel would have been like in the time of Offa. It first of all passes through the forestry plantation surrounding Pendinas Reservoir (235517), and in fact it is possible to make a slight diversion from the path, and to follow the track down to the reservoir itself.

Once through the plantation, the route follows the track south along some extremely wild moorland to the appropriately named World's End (233479). The path then runs parallel with the road that skirts the edge of the great geological fault of Eglwyseg Mountain (221463).

The section of walk around Trevor Uchaf (246428) is wonderful. It follows a series of wooded valleys, chiselled out of rolling hills dotted with sheep. Behind are the giant terraces of Eglwyseg rocks. From here the walk crosses the River Dee and heads south to join Offa's Dyke itself.

Survivals of another earthwork known as Wat's Dyke can also be seen and walked along. Not much is known of the Dyke, but it is thought to be an earlier prototype of Offa's Dyke, serving the same purpose. It is still visible at Vownog (250661), on the northern outskirts of Wrexham (334530), and there is a particularly well preserved section near Hafad House (321460).

Modern Footpaths: The Chester and Wrexham area is a superb area for walking, and a number of modern paths and trails have been developed to show off the beauty of the countryside. One of the best is the Sandstone Trail, developed by the Cheshire County Council, which stretches along the eastern edge of the area.

The walk begins at Beacon Hill, Frodsham (518771) and offers good views back to Frodsham and across to the Manchester Ship Canal. From the hill the walk heads south through the picturesque Delamere Forest (542713), where there are numerous picnic sites to be enjoyed.

From the forest the walk crosses the farmland of the Beeston Gap and Wharton's Lock over the Shropshire Union Canal (539602), before passing the remains of Beeston Castle (539593). Beyond the castle the scenery changes once more as the route climbs the wooded Peckforton Hills. The rocky outcrop at Raw Head (507548) stands at 746 feet high, and is the highest point of the walk.

After passing the curiously named Mad Allen's Hole, another range of hills must be climbed. But in contrast to the Peckforton Hills, those at Bickerton are heather covered (500522). This is quite a strenuous part of the trail, and thankfully the final stretch is a descent to the farmland of Willey Moor, and then finally a stroll along the Llangollen branch of the Shropshire Union Canal to Grindley Brook (521433).

The Sandstone Trail is a good walk for introducing the stranger to the varying landscapes of the Welsh borders. However, there are a number of other fine walks in the region, such as around Cholmondeley Castle (537516), Combermere Park (585436) and along the banks of the River Dee at Connah's Quay (310692).

Climber's Crags at Helsby Hill (Ref: 4975. Picture: D. Pratt)

In Roman times, Whitchurch (5441) was the half-way stage for the journey from Chester (Roman name, Deva) to Wroxeter (Viroconium, map 126) and was known as Mediolanum (*medio* half). Excavated Roman remains are now on view in the Whitchurch Museum. The town had a church built of white stone in Norman or medieval times and this gave rise to the town name which we now use. Being in the centre of a rich agricultural area, this is an ancient market town and has all the associated trades. Near the church are the Higginson Almshouses of 1647, built of brick in the Georgian style. Between the town centre and the modern ring road, there are the old primary school and the old grammar school of the 18th and 19th century respectively. Barclays Bank uses the old Market Hall and Lloyd's Bank is a Georgian, ie it was built between 1714 and 1830, when Kings George I to IV reigned. The post office occupies the former Methodist chapel, the National Westminster Bank and W. H. Smith use timber-framed buildings and the former workhouse changed function to be a hospital. Whitchurch is making excellent use of its historic buildings.

Chester is a settlement of great antiquity on a red sandstone outcrop, on the north bank of a loop in the River Dee. A natural crossing place, it was a site favourable for defence. The Romans used the river bank, now the racecourse, as the site of their port, a sign of their commercial ingenuity and prosperity, and built a huge (100m square) amphitheatre east of Newgate, a sign of a large population in the area and their intention to remain. The large town which they built they fortified and encircled with substantial walls up to 10m high and three km in circumference. The wall is still largely intact despite the follies of local planners and the insatiable demands of the motorist. However, there have been earlier alterations to the wall, for instance, the south and west sections were moved outwards to increase the enclosed area but whether this was done by the Romans, Anglo-Saxons or Normans is uncertain because the original stone was re-used. King Charles' Tower at the north-east corner of the wall, the subject of post Norman restorations, is now a museum displaying a Civil War (1642–49) exhibition. Following the withdrawal of the Romans in 410, invading tribes caused the destruction of some of the Roman buildings but in late Anglo-Saxon times the city was sufficiently prosperous to operate its own mint. Normans arriving by 1070 built a castle and continued the city's commercial revival but when the last surviving Norman earl died in the 13th century the city became the property of the Crown and, still, each monarch's eldest son is the Earl of Chester.

The original Roman street plan of Chester with routes to north, east, south and west remains – upper Northgate Street, Eastgate Street, Foregate Street, Bridge Street and Watergate Street, some of which still lead to former Roman

The Rows, Chester (Picture: D. Pratt)

roads outside the city to the east and south. The restoration of the town in medieval times included the building of unique tiers of shops now named *The Rows* with shops at pavement and first floor levels and a first floor continuous balcony serving as the first floor pavement. Tudor and Elizabethan construction followed and may still be found. In Watergate there is Bishop Lloyd's House which despite early 20th century restoration is the best example. Lloyd was Bishop from 1604–15 and his brother also served the community as Lord Mayor 1593–4. Leche House is 15th century with 17th century restoration and is regarded as the least changed building. John Leche was leachman (surgeon) to Edward III. Stanley Place built in 1591 is another magnificent timbered building. It became the townhouse of the Stanley family, and God's Providence House adjoins but both are much restored. In Bridge Street inns abound. The Old King's Head of the 17th century possibly refers to King Charles I who had watched Civil War battles from the city walls in 1645. The Falcon of 1626, the Bear and Billet of 1664 and Gamul House are other old buildings. Eastgate and its continuation is largely Victorian but in Tudor style whilst Northgate has a Roman hypocaust (a Roman basement room fed with hot air to heat the room above) in the basement of a popular store. Notice also the Victorian Town Hall of 1867, the Bluecoat School and the almshouses. The Cheshire Military Museum is, significantly, housed in the Castle and exhibits items relating to the Cheshire Regiment and others. The Grosvenor Museum has rooms devoted to the Roman, Anglo-Saxon, Georgian and Victorian eras. Mystery Plays based on biblical stories originated in the 14th century and are still given triennially in the cathedral precincts. In the 16th century the Shoemakers' Company played football against the Drapers' Company but injuries were sustained and the event changed to footraces and then to horse racing on the Roodee. This is the origin of this famous race course. Boating on the river is popular and recalls the trace of the Chester port until it was closed by 14th century silting. At that time the Lord Mayor was also Admiral of the Dee and his prowess is reflected in the present custom of the Lord Mayor judging the annual Head of the River Race. Chester Zoo (4170) has a large collection of animals as unobtrusively enclosed as is consistent with safety. Chester is a delight and its names are historically interesting. The Romans used our local name of the river – Deva – for their town, whilst we use a derivative of the Roman name for a camp – castra – for ours.

Delamere Forest (5471) – the forest of the meres (lakes) – is the remnant of a huge royal hunting forest owned by the Earls of Chester from Norman times. The area is threaded with public footpaths including the Red Sandstone Way which commences at Frodsham (5278). There is a Forestry Commission Visitor Centre which describes its history and current management.

Ness Gardens (3075) on the red sandstone ridge, were commenced in 1898 by a successful Liverpool cotton broker, Kilpin Bulley, who introduced species of foreign plants in large numbers to form a very extensive and rare collection. These he developed commercially, forming Bees Seeds Ltd. Soon after his death in 1942, the estate was donated to Liverpool University and it is used as a research station and may be viewed.

Stretton Mill (4553) dates from the 14th century and was bought by the Leche family in 1596 when it was a timber and thatch building. It was rebuilt with stone, timber and slate in the 17th century. Successive generations of the family ground corn here until 1959 since when it has been made into a working museum.

Malpas (4847) lies on the Roman road from Chester to Whitchurch and is a small, largely unchanged market town of some antiquity with timbered and medieval brick houses. Conveniently off the main road from the south to Chester it was, however, not bypassed by the Parliamentary forces in the Civil War who effected much damage in the town and fought at Oldcastle Heath to the southwest. The old Market House, of brick, is nearly 300 years old and has ground floor Tuscan columns of stone and is now used as a commercial establishment. Church Street has a prized row of 18th century almshouses founded by the Earl of Cholmondeley and with the family arms displayed in the central pediment.

Ellesmere Port (4077) in Cheshire, originated as a port where the Ellesmere canal from Ellesmere in Shropshire (map 126) entered the River Mersey. at Ellesmere Port, Thomas Telford built warehouses and workshops some of which are now the Ellesmere Port Boat Museum. This canal became a hub of the national canal system.

Wrexham (3350) was a small but important medieval market town serving the rural areas of the Welsh valleys to the west and the extension of the Cheshire plain to the east until the advent of the Industrial Revolution during the 18th century. Coal mining and iron smelting were introduced, together with the associated trades, including brewing. The town increased slowly in size from a population of 2,500 in 1800 to 15,000 in 1900. This change is reflected in the buildings of which the church is a good example. The nave arcades are of the 14th century with a celebrated 16th century tower. The County Buildings of 1856 were built as militia barracks and converted to magistrates' courts and a police station in 1879, following the opening of Hightown Barracks in 1877, and now are used as council offices. The infirmary of 1838 is now the College of Art. The market hall (for butchers) is of 1848 and near it is the general market of 1879. There are many public buildings of the post-WWII era.

Llangollen (2142) is world famous for its International Eisteddfod which began in 1948 to present competitively international song, folk dance and music to foster peace. It receives much support from competing teams from home and overseas and is highly enjoyed and respected. The festival is held annually in July.

Ellesmere Port Boat Museum (Ref: 4077. Picture: Ellesmere Port Boat Museum)

13

The inner reaches of the Dee estuary are heavily industrialised, offering nothing for the visitor interested in bathing beaches. The mudbanks are an unappealing prospect and the swirling currents rule out swimming. However, there are some pleasant spots and much of historical interest along the coastline.

Neston, once the largest town in the Wirrall, offers an attractive shoreline walk including excellent views over the estuary to the Welsh mountains. The footpath stretches from nearby Burton (315745) through Neston to Parkgate before joining the route of the Wirrall Country Park which, following an old railway line, extends along the length of the peninsula. Ness, the village neighbouring Neston, was the birthplace of Lady Emma Hamilton.

The history of the small towns along the Dee estuary is that of the battle between man and nature. As the estuary gradually silted up, these towns were used as ports for Chester. Parkgate was once one such bustling and important harbour, taking over Chester's trade with Ireland. The sands won the battle here too and the mudflats around Parkgate now attract a wide variety of birds.

The Clwyd side of the estuary is more industrial. Connah's Quay, previously used as an alternative port when Chester became unreachable, is now the site of other industries and a power station.

Flint, another old port, is still renowned for its castle, built in 1277 by Edward I, his first in Wales. It was the setting for Shakespeare's dramatisation of Richard II's pitiful surrender to Bolingbroke in 1399. It was in this flat and desolate landscape that Richard resolved to:

> *Go to Flint castle, there I'll pine away –*
> *A King, woe's slave, shall kingly woe obey:"*

There is little left of "the rude ribs of that ancient castle," today, but the basic plan is still visible. Edward also designed the town on a gridiron pattern, which Flint's nineteenth century terraces still largely follow.

Opportunities for sailing and swimming do not improve to the west of Flint. The sandbanks of Bagilt Bank and the strong currents surrounding it, together with the muddy foreshore make swimming impossible. However the saltings along these shores are much more rewarding for the walker, birdwatcher, or local historian.

Ellesmere Port (Picture: D. Pratt)

PLACE NAMES

English place-names exist in layers, each associated with a stage in the development of English history.

The earliest layer of names on English maps dates from the arrival of the Celts about three thousand years ago. These names are more common in the North and West. Then, after the Roman occupation, it was the coming of the Angles and Saxons (5th to 7th centuries) which provided the chief source of place-names. Finally a layer of Scandinavian names was given to parts of North and East England by the Danish conquests (9th century) and the raids of the Norsemen (10th century).

When the Normans arrived in 1066 English place-names were largely fixed. Since then, although often varying in spelling and pronunciation throughout the centuries, the root elements have remained the same.

Chester (400670) is the "Roman fort". *Wrexham* (340510) is "Wrythel's meadow by the river".

Ellesmere Port (400760) takes its name from the *Ellesmere* (Shropshire Union) *Canal* which,

The local pub sign at Minera recalls the village's lead mining days
(Ref: 2758. Picture: A. Burton)

Restored horse gin at Bersham (Ref: 3049. Picture: A. Burton)

in turn, received it from *Ellesmere* in Shropshire (400350 on Landranger Map 126). The meaning is "Elli's mere" or "lake".

Mold (240640) is the "high hill" from the Old French *mont-hault*. *Neston* (290770) is the "farm on the headland", *Helsby* (490750) is the "farm on the side of a hill", *Frodsham* (520780) is "Frod's homestead", and *Farndon* (415543) is the "ferny hill".

Tilston (459515) is "Tilli's farm", *Tilstone Fearnall* (566604) is "Tidwulf's stone at the ferny place", *Burton* (315743) is the "fortified manor", *Flint* (240720) is the "place of the hard stone" and *Malpas* (488472) is the "place of the difficult passage". *Saughall* (360700) is the "remote place where the sallows grow" and *Tarvin* (490665) is named from the *River Tarvin* which name comes from the Welsh *terfyn* or "boundary".

Christleton (442655) is the "village with a cross", *Waverton* (455642) is the "farm in the brushwood", *Rowton* (447643) is an abbreviated form of "Rough Christleton" and *Churton* (418565) is "church farm". The place-name element *ton* comes from the Old English *tun* which can mean variously "enclosure", "farmstead", "manor" or "village". It was possible for a *tun* to expand through all these phases of development whilst keeping the same name.

Threapwood (440455) is the "disputed wood", *Whitchurch* (540415) is the "white church" and *Burwardsley* (514566) is "Burgweard's wood".

In waterway terms, this map has everything, from broad rivers to narrow canals. In the north, the Wirral Peninsula separates two important river systems: the Mersey, into which flows the Weaver, and the Dee. Although today we think of the Mersey as the great shipping river of the North West, historically the Dee takes precedence. Chester was an important port in Roman times, and remained so for many centuries. But by the end of the seventeenth century, a commentator was writing that "the Trade of Chester is much decayed, and gone to Liverpool". The tidal Dee is an extremely difficult river to negotiate, and should not be attempted without a pilot by anyone who does not know it well. In Chester itself the river is spanned by a weir (407658) which can only be crossed by boats at certain conditions of the tide and can only be used by prior arrangement. Above the weir, the river is an altogether more manageable affair and a variety of vessels use it as far as the bridge (412544) that links Farndon in England to Holt in Wales. It is an attractive, fourteenth century bridge over a very attractive river: the other appealing bridge is at Aldford (417601), an ornate affair in cast iron, built in 1824 to carry the driveway to Eaton Hall. Below Farndon, the river can be used by small, shallow draught craft, while the upper Welsh reaches offer demanding white-water canoeing for experts.

Chester is now linked to the main canal system of Britain via the Shropshire Union Canal which, as its name suggests, is not one canal but a group joined together at a later date. Three of them appear on this map: the Chester, the Ellesmere and the Birmingham and Liverpool Junction. The first to be built was the Chester Canal itself. It was begun very early in the canal age in 1772 and was built to generous dimensions, for it was intended for use by river barges, up to 13ft 2ins beam. It was not, however, a great success initially. The idea was to join Chester to Nantwich and on to the Trent and Mersey Canal at Middlewich. Sadly, it reached Nantwich in 1779, but stuck there for another half century. Later developments restored its fortunes, and it is now both an interesting and sometimes dramatic waterway. It enters the map at 600580, and after two kilometres arrives at Bunbury locks. This is a two-lock staircase,

in which the upper lock empties straight into the one below, and there is a reminder of the days when horses pulled the boats in the lockside stables. Beyond this is a pleasing, rural canal that wanders along until the sharp descent into Chester. First there are memories of trading days in the area of wharves and warehouses, then an older Chester appears as the canal creeps round the edge of the city walls which rise sheer above it. After that there is a sudden plunge of 10 metres down a 3-lock staircase carved out of the sandstone – again as at Bunbury, the locks inter-connect. Beyond that is the old company headquarters and broad locks connecting into the Dee.

The Chester Canal's revival came when new connections were made, beginning near Nantwich, with the Ellesmere Canal. This is probably the most popular pleasure boating canal in the country, though few recognise it by the old name. It is known, instead, by what the original engineers regarded as a mere branch line, the route to Llangollen. It was built to pass through the market town of Ellesmere and to lead to the important ironworks around Ruabon in North Wales. Work began in 1793, under the direction of the engineer, William Jessop. It appears first at 600478. At first it is a pleasant, if undramatic waterway, but as the contour lines begin to crowd together, so the nature of the canal begins to change. At Grindley Brook (5243) the canal rises steeply through six locks, three of which are joined together in a staircase. After that evasive action is taken, and the canal twists through a hairpin bend to avoid the next hill. It leaves the map at 518400 but reappears at 286400, emerging from the short tunnel.

Reaching the valley of the Dee, the canal turns sharply to the west, carried high on a massive embankment before turning north again to cross the river on the great aqueduct, Pontcysyllte.

There was much discussion about this river crossing, but before work started, Jessop's assistant, an engineer at the beginning of his career, Thomas Telford, was seconded away to complete another canal in Shropshire, and there he used a new technique for the crossing of the River Tern: an aqueduct with an iron trough. It seemed the ideal solution here as well, and together Jessop, Telford and William Hazeldine of the nearby Plas Kynaston Ironworks planned the greatest canal structure in Britain. Nineteen stone arches carry the iron trough for over 300 metres, at the giddy height of 37 metres above the Dee. Pontcysyllte by boat or on foot is a unique experience.

The main line then ran on a little way to the north, but to supply the canal with water, a feeder was constructed to take water from the Dee, west of Llangollen. It is a narrow, navigable channel that hugs the hillside and is used by boats as far as Llangollen, though small craft can continue on to the end. At Llangollen itself there is a canal museum (215421) which is also the starting point for passenger trips on horse-drawn boats on this most beautiful canal.

In 1826, Telford returned to this area as chief engineer of the Birmingham and Liverpool Junction Canal. This new route used the old Chester Canal and extended it south and north. The northern section ended at a brand new dock complex, Ellesmere Port. Sadly, many of the old warehouses were

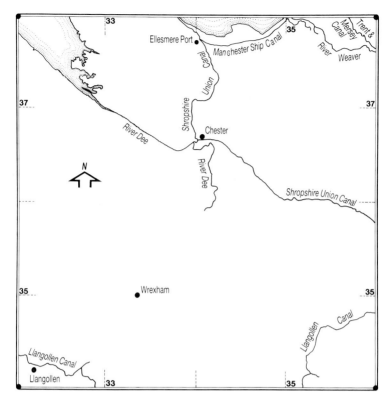

Navigable waterways

destroyed by fire, but the remainder are now the basis of the Boat Museum (405772). Here are waterways craft of all kinds: not just the famous narrow boats of the type that once used the old Telford Canal, but barges of all kinds and vessels as large as a 300-ton coaster. There are exhibitions in the old buildings, many preserved features and boat trips for visitors.

Ellesmere Port's importance

increased immeasurably with the construction of the Manchester Ship Canal at the end of the nineteenth century, which enabled large vessels to go to the heart of that city. It can be seen appearing at 376800 and the Ellesmere Port docks are still very much in use.

The other major waterway that links into the Ship Canal is the River Weaver, which is now one of the few British River Navigations to have benefited from extensive modernisation, which began in the 1870s when the locks were trebled in size, so that now 500-ton coasters can use the river, which leaves the map at 600762.

Finally, there is a brief appearance of the canal which the Chester was originally planned to join, the Trent and Mersey. This was Britain's first real trunk route, begun in 1766 under the direction of James Brindley and completed in 1777. It appears at 600765 on the hillside above the Weaver and disappears into the 1133 metre long Preston Brook tunnel at 573787.

There is no Anglo-Saxon church in Cheshire but there are some crosses. In the area of this map there are fragments of crosses at Chester Church of St. John and Neston Church of St. Mary and St. Helen.

Frodsham (5277) Church of St. Laurence has a traditional plan of chancel with a north chapel, nave with north and south aisles and a west tower. The chancel is 14th and 15th century. The north chancel chapel is 16th century. The nave west end of the north arcade, and the north aisle and clerestory are Norman. The south aisle was rebuilt in the 19th century. In the tower south wall there are fragments of stone and sculpture which are probably Saxon. As one travels through unpretentious Frodsham one wonders why it has been so favoured as to have and to have retained such church treasures as are noted here.

Chester Cathedral is the church of a former Benedictine abbey, the building of which commenced in 1092. It is difficult to interpret the architectural detail because there are few original documents and there were three restorations in the 19th century, following those of previous centuries.

At the east end there is a 13th century lady chapel. The choir and its south aisle were restored in the 19th century. The south transept has 14–16th century features. The north transept is Norman. The crossing tower is 16th century, the nave has a 14th century aisle and a 16th century clerestory. The base of the southwest tower and the south porch are 16th century. The northwest tower is Norman but is obscured by a commercial bank which occupies the building previously used by the King's School. This is on the site of the former bishop's palace which had previously been the abbot's lodging. The north tower is Norman. The choir stalls have carving of unusually high quality and are of the 14th century. The dean's and the vice-dean's stalls are especially good. The chalice is of 1496. In the area of the monastic buildings there is the south wall of the cloister which is the north wall of the cathedral nave and this is Norman. The 12th century Norman Chapel of St. Anselm, with three bays, adjoins the site of the abbot's lodging. The monastery was dissolved in 1540 at the Dissolution of the Monasteries and the church was made a cathedral in 1541.

Eastgate Tower, Chester
(Picture: D. Pratt)

The Church of St. John has Saxon origins and was refounded by Leofric, Earl of Mercia in 1057, just before the invasion by the Normans. It was made a cathedral in 1075 soon after the arrival of the Normans in Chester but only until 1095 when the see was moved again, to Coventry. The first bay of the chancel, the crossing and the nave are Norman. The organ was first used in Westminster Abbey for Queen Victoria's Coronation in 1837 but the organ case is from much later.

The Roman Catholic Church of St. Francis in Grosvenor Street, built in 1874–5 and designed by J. O'Byrne, is unusually wide and without aisles or tower.

Beeston Castle (5359) was built by Randle Blundeville, Earl of Chester in 1220 and on his death in 1237 it reverted to the possession of the Crown in whose ownership it has remained. It was extended by Henry III and Edward II. It is situated on a steep-sided natural hill of 100m. There is an

Valle Crucis Abbey (Ref: 208440. Picture: A. Burton)

upper enclosure with a strong 13th century gatehouse, with two towers, and a lower bailey with parts of the outer gatehouse and seven circular towers. By the time of the Civil War the castle was already in ruins.

Flint Castle (2473) was the first castle built by Edward I in Wales and was begun in 1227. The enclosure wall has a tower at each corner with the southeast tower being larger than the others. This included living accommodation and the chapel on the upper floors. The outer bailey and the south moat were all subject to tidal water from the River Dee. Much of the castle was demolished after being surrendered to the Parliamentarians in 1646 and the Flintshire County Gaol was erected in the outer ward in 1785 but removed in 1969.

Erddig (3248) is a brick-built house built in 1680 by Thomas Webb for Joshua Edisbury. Peter Yorke who inherited the property in 1767 had the west front refaced and the park landscaped by William Emes and this is one of the joys of the house – the setting in sloping parkland with scattered trees and rolling fields. The next joy is the inside of the house. The second owner, John Meller, a London lawyer, was an avid collector of tapestries, oriental porcelain, furniture and silver and he left all of it to a nephew, Simon Yorke in 1733, since when the house has belonged to the family until 1973 when the property was gifted to the National Trust. Little was discarded during the Yorkes' ownership and all is revealed for visitors. A special attraction is the opportunity to see the workshops of the trades of the estate – smithy, saw pit, laundries, bakehouse etc.

Eaton Hall (4160) was the Gothic palace built for the first Duke of Westminster in 1873. Though much was demolished in 1965, numerous buildings in the park and in surrounding villages remain and provide a social and architectural history of the estate in the 19th century. The Hall has been replaced by a modern house designed by Ove Arup. Eaton came into the possession of the Grosvenors in the 15th century. The first house here was built in 1683 for Sir Thomas Grosvenor, third baronet. He married the heiress of the manor of Ebury who owned land in Mayfair and Belgravia, then being developed and this is the origin of the family wealth. The 7th baronet was made Baron Grosvenor in 1761 and Viscount Belgrave and Earl Grosvenor in 1784.

Eccleston (4162) is regarded as the prettiest of the Eaton Hall estate villages. The Church of St. Mary was rebuilt in 1899 by the 1st Duke of Westminster and is of Perpendicular (14th century) style with a chancel, nave and west tower adorned with much decoration and beautiful furniture and flooring. There are remains in the churchyard of a church built in 1813 and demolished in 1900. The village school of 1878 is small and decorated with a turret and spire. The village pumphouse was built in 1874 and near the southwest corner of the churchyard there is a small half-timbered cottage and a carriage shed and barn, all of 1870 – the latter now a residence. The manor house of 1632 is now divided into small units.

This is a busy and complex railway map, which appears at first glance to be focused on two centres, Chester and Wrexham, but this is only partly the case. The first, and most important, line only features briefly on the map, cutting across from 568800 to 600745. This was the Grand Junction Railway, begun in 1833 to join the recently completed Liverpool and Manchester to the London and Birmingham, authorised on the same day. The route was surveyed by Joseph Locke, and the role of engineer was briefly shared be-tween him and George Stephenson, before the latter dropped out. The line also saw the first appearance of a young contractor, Thomas Brassey, who was to go on to build railways throughout the world. The line has one notable feature, the Dutton viaduct across the Weaver (582764).

The Grand Junction soon threw out branches, and the first to appear was from what was to become the first town called into being by the railways, Crewe. The Chester and Crewe, which can be

Coal train at Minera, 1890 (Picture: Clwyd Record Office)

seen appearing at 600583, closely following the line of the Shropshire Union Canal, was absorbed into the Grand Junction even before its opening in 1840. Again Brassey was involved, but this time under the direction of Robert Stephenson. At the same time, work was going ahead on a line connecting Chester to Birkenhead, a line of which the Grand Junction took a very poor view, since it offered an alternative, shorter route to Liverpool via the ferry. This is the line leaving the map at 345800. Chester now had two railways, two stations – and a gap across which the rival companies glared at each other.

The next line of major importance to leave Chester was the line to Holyhead, built once again under the direction of Robert Stephenson. It was opened as far as Bangor in 1848, and the section shown here, leaving the map at 200776, presented few engineering problems other than the viaduct at Chester. This was built of cast iron, which proved to be an inappropriate material when it suddenly

The restored Hadlow Road Station on the Wirral Way (Picture: A. Burton)

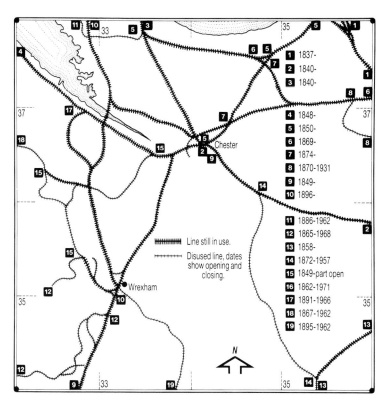

The railway network, past and present

collapsed shortly after completion with the loss of five lives. Meanwhile amalgamations were in the offing. The Great Western Railway (GWR) was threatening to expand north from its home in the south west, and to meet that threat, the Grand Junction, London and Birmingham and some lesser lines joined to form the London and North Western Railway (LNWR) in 1846. One result was a splendid new station for Chester.

Another company joined the fray in 1846, the Birkenhead, Lancashire and Cheshire Junction Railway, which runs from Hooton (352776) to 543800 en route for Warrington and its eventual destination, the Manchester and Birmingham. Eventually, this was modified and the line progressed only as far as a junction near

Warrington. There was a branch from Helsby (487755) to Chester. Then the West Cheshire Railway appeared, building a line west out of Northwich which might have been expected to head for Chester but instead veered north to join the Birkenhead line at Helsby. It joins the map at 600716, following a somewhat erratic course. Chester was eventually given a direct line from the Junction at Mickle Trafford (447694). In 1862, a branch was authorised to the saltworks at Winsford: now disused, it leaves the map at 600688. The old line is now the Whitegate Way. Walkers can use the whole route, but horse riders are restricted to the section east of Kennel Lane (593692). The lagoon by Kennel Lane is used by Canada Geese for breeding. The five mile route is continued on Sheet 118.

The focus now shifts south to the lines through Wrexham. An early appearance was put in by the Shrewsbury and Chester line, the route that was eventually to give the GWR its access to the region. This is the line joining the map at 286400. It was opened in 1848 and absorbed six years later. This was not the only take-over to affect the region. The next line running north from Wrexham was a hybrid, which began as two quite distinct lines: the Wrexham, Mold and Connah's Quay from 330519, which was to meet another complex system, consisting of the branch line from Chester to Connah's Quay and a new route down from Birkenhead, joining the map at 287800. The line went through various names, until it was absorbed by the Great Central Railway in 1905. In 1886, a branch line from Hooton was built to run round to the edge of the Dee estuary, the disused line leaving the map at 270800.

This last line now forms the core of the Wirral Country Park, a foot-path and bridle way from Hooton to West Kirby (Sheet 108). It has one great advantage for walkers – Hooton and West Kirby are still connected by rail, completing a round trip of the peninsula. The walk combines the pleasures of the estuary, with its mud flats and wading birds, with green, shady cuttings. Hadlow Road station (330773) has been beautifully restored to look much as it did when the last train picked up the last passenger here in 1956. Track has been laid, level crossing gates are in place and the home signal is set to stop. Milk churns await collection on the platform, the booking hall is overlooked by the faded pictures of old railwaymen and the signal box stands ready for use. It is hard to believe that no train will ever come.

Returning to the south, there is a disused line running from a junction south of Ruabon, leaving the map beyond Llangollen at 200432. The line was opened to Llangollen in 1861 and extended to Corwen in 1865, eventually running all the way to Dolgellau and Barmouth in 1868. This was yet another line for which the contractor was Thomas Brassey, and it was in time to form a part of the great GWR empire. It too has found a new role, at least in part, as a preserved steam railway, the only standard gauge preserved line in Wales. At present there are two miles of track open, west from Llangollen, but there are plans to re-open the line to Corwen. The emphasis is very much on GWR locomotives, from a 1918 2-8-0 to two examples of the popular "Manor" class. It is a short, but scenically delightful riverside run, that can only get better with the steady extension of the line.

The working line that cuts across the south eastern corner through Whitchurch is the Shrews-bury and Crewe, developed with the very active encouragement of the LNWR – yet another Brassey line. The branch line that ran from Whitchurch (551420) to the Chester and Crewe at 472620 was a less than satisfactory affair, which opened in 1872 and closed with few mourners in 1957.

The Shrewsbury and Chester Railway planned a branch to Mold (2364) but it was actually built by a separate Mold Railway, which added a branch to limeworks at Ffrith (2855). Opened in 1849, and worked by the LNWR, it was a daunting line, which included a section with a 1 in 43 incline near Higher Kinnerton (3260). The LNWR built an experimental 0-6-0 goods tender locomotive to cope with it – a design which led to the very successful DX class. South of Ffrith, the area was served at first by the Wrexham and Minera Railway, opened in 1862. Eventually, the system all came together as the Wrexham and Minera Joint Railway.

The Mold and Denbigh Junction Railway, the disused route leaving the Map at 200676 had an unhappy start. Authorised in 1861, it was not taken up by the giant LNWR and had to look to private finance, which ran out just as the line was almost complete. Nevertheless trains did run into Denbigh in 1867. The final link in the rail system round Wrexham came with the construction of the Wrexham and Ellesmere Railway, opened in 1895 and closed in 1962. It leaves the map at 387400.

The Town Crier, Chester (Picture: D. Pratt)

There are surprisingly few very ancient remains on this map, though the Iron Age that lasted from c. 500 BC to the Roman invasion is well represented. The characteristic survival of the period was the hill fort in which the natural defences offered by steep slopes were improved by digging ditches round the crown of the hill and using the spoil to build up ramparts. Castle Ditch Fort on Eddisbury Hill (553695) has a double rampart. It was dismantled in the 1st century AD by the Romans who built a road out from Chester alongside it. Maiden Castle (497528) is a promontory fort: the sheer cliffs to the north west required no extra earthwork, but elsewhere there were double ramparts, the inner built of stone, laced together with timbers. The entrance was through a long cobbled passageway which narrowed down from 5 metres to 2.4 metres. There are other, but less impressive, forts at Helsby Hill (492754) and Kelsborrow Castle (531675).

Chester was the Roman town of Deva. It became the fortress of the

Rossett Mill, Rossett, Clwyd (Ref: 3657. Picture: D. Widdicombe)

Amphitheatre at Chester (Picture: D. Widdicombe)

2nd legion and later of the 20th legion. It stood at the centre of a network of roads and a port was established on the Dee: part of the quay wall can be seen by the racecourse, Roodee (400656). The remains of part of the big amphitheatre, able to hold 8000 people, can be seen at Newgate (408662). There are remains of columns and sections of hypocaust which can be seen from the walk round the town walls. There is an impressive collection of finds in Grosvenor Museum. The city walls themselves are well preserved and include King Charles' Tower, originally built in the thirteenth century. It was here that the King stood in 1645 to watch the defeat of his army at the Battle of Rowton Moor.

The great survivor from the Dark Ages is Offa's Dyke, built by Offa, King of Mercia, AD 757–96. It was built as a defence against the Britons who had been pushed west into what is now Wales, and it runs from the Bristol Channel to the Dee estuary. It is not at its most impressive in this area, but it can be traced northwards from 298483 by the B5097. The Pillar of Eliseg (203445) commemorates the life of Eliseg, a contemporary and bitter opponent of Offa. It was erected by his grandson who died in Rome in AD 854, and its Latin inscription, now obliterated, recorded his lineage, and that of the kings of Powys. Nearby is the thirteenth century Cistercian abbey of Valle Crucis (204442). The remains are substantial, starting with the fine west end, with its thirteenth century door.

The estuaries of the Dee and, perhaps more surprisingly, the Mersey (the dirtiest estuary in Britain) are both noted haunts of wildfowl, especially in winter. On the Dee, the RSPB reserve of Gayton Sands (274786) forms a huge area of saltmarsh (with plants such as glasswort, scurvy grass and sea aster), sandbanks and mudflats. This, in winter, supports large numbers of knot, dunlin, curlew, redshank, oyster-catchers and grey plover amongst the waders, whilst wildfowl include pintail and many shelduck, mallard, wigeon and teal. The salt-marsh plants attract seed-eating finches and buntings, including brambling and generally a few twite. In turn, these bring in hen harriers, merlins, peregrines and short-eared owls to hunt over the saltmarsh.

East and north from Neston, a disused railway line forms the Wirral Country Park, and for much of its length it overlooks the Dee estuary (273796). The linear park also has large hedgerows, open embankments and wooded areas, with a good variety of wildlife.

Although Cheshire is a little-wooded county, there is an extensive area of Forestry Commission conifer plantations at Delamere Forest (540715). The many walks through the forest will reveal good bird populations, including pied flycatchers, long-eared owls, cross-bills and occasional buzzards. There are also a number of small lakes, the margins of which support bog plants such as cranberry, cottongrass and sundew; Hatch-mere (553721) is a good example.

The Cheshire Sandstone Trail
links Delamere to the Peckforton Hills. These are again well-wooded, with both plantations and native woodland of oak, birch and rowan. The southernmost, Bickerton Hill, (498529) also has areas of heath-land, with both heather and bil-berry, though there is much encroachment by oak and birch trees.

Heather-dominated habitats are generally known as heathlands in the lowlands and moorland in upland areas. This area, on the borders of Wales and England, can claim to have both represented.

A plant resembling large rhubarb leaves gowing in extensive patches by streams and marshes is likely to be butterbur. In the early spring, even before the leaves appear, stout spikes of reddish pink flowers may be seen growing close to the ground. Butterbur is found throughout Britiain in wet places.

The Shropshire Union Canal, near Chester Zoo (Ref: 413712. Picture: D. Pratt)

Clwyd County Council's Waun-y-Llyn Country Park (284577) is upland moorland with peat bogs and a small lake. Mynydd Eglwyseg (233485) is also moorland, accessible along rights of way though still managed as a grouse shoot. In this case, the expanses of heather and bilberry are varied with cross-leaved heath and bog vegetation including sundews in wetter areas, bell heather in drier places and flowers such as tormentil scattered about. To the west, the edge of the moor is marked by impressive limestone cliffs which support a different range of vegetation – wild thyme, herb robert and maidenhair spleenwort are amongst the plants which grow here.

Between the cliffs and the town from which it gets its name, the Llangollen Canal provides a haven for wetland wildlife. Coots and moorhens nest on its margins, herons and kingfishers feed there, and dragonflies and water voles are also in evidence. Colourful bankside flowers include kingcups, cuckooflower, water forgetmenot, meadowsweet and a bright yellow introduction from North America, the monkeyflower.

At Tan-y-cut Wood (282411) there is a nature trail between the canal and the Dee, through damp woodland with giant horsetail, pendulous sedge and the huge leaves of butterbur. The North Wales Wildlife Trust manage another area of wet alder woodland with plants such as guelder rose and hemlock water dropwort at Hafod Wood (324477). This is on the National Trust's Erddig Park estate.

The south west corner of this map was once the scene of intense industrial activity; there was coal mining, lead mining and smelting and, most importantly, iron making and iron working. The Bersham Industrial Heritage Centre (310493) has been developed in the area where John Wilkinson had his ironworks. His greatest achievement was the invention of a machine for accurately boring cannon, which was to find a far more important application in boring cylinders for the steam engines of Boulton and Watt. His story is told in the museum. The other iron works featured are very different. The Davies Brothers had a forge to the south of Bersham where they produced wrought iron work of great artistry: the gates of Chirk Castle (Sheet 126) being their masterpiece. Other exhibits include a reconstruction of a mine horse gin, where a horse plodding round a circle heaved men and materials up and down the shaft.

Bersham is the starting point for the Bersham and Clywedog Industrial Trail. This takes in the still active Brymbo steelworks (2953) where the remains of an old nineteenth century blast furnace can still be seen. At Minera City Mine the old lead mine site is marked by the engine house (274511) that once held the beam engine that carried material up and down the shaft. The name is preserved in the nearby City Arms pub which shows the engine house in its working days.

Much of the rest of the area is agricultural, and has a number of watermills, where the waterwheels turn the grindstones that turn grain into flour. Stretton Mill (454530) is a delightful small working mill. Water is stored in a mill pond, from which it can be directed to an overshot wheel. This is one in which the water falls onto the top of the wheel, filling "buckets" round the rim, so that the weight causes the wheel to turn. A similar arrangement can be seen at Bunbury mill (575581). The most attractive mill in the area can be seen beside the bridge that carries the A483 over the Alyn at Rossett (365572). The building is half timbered and carries the date 1661 on the façade, though it is probably older. Here the wheel is undershot: it is turned by the force of water hitting paddles on the rim. King's Mill of 1769 (345491) is currently being restored. The Erddig Visitor Centre is part of the Erddig Estate (326482). Housed in

City Lead Mine, Minera, c 1905
(Picture: Clwyd Record Office)

a seventeenth century barn, it has a collection of farm machinery and exhibits showing changes on the estate.

There are two museums of a scientific rather than an industrial nature. Bwlchgwyn (259533) is a geological museum, where the rock garden is literally just that. There is also a geological trail, using an old quarry to display the features, such as strata and rock types. Liverpool University's Botanic Gardens (3075) are beautiful gardens in themselves and there are exhibitions in the Visitors Centre.

Chester is a city with a rich history, much of which is told in the Heritage Centre, housed in the former St. Michael's Church in the city centre at Bridge Street Row. The Grosvenor Museum incorporates the Georgian House in Castle Street, but the main exhibitions are in the museum of 1886 in Grosvenor Street.

The Manchester Ship Canal at Ince (Ref: 4577. Picture: D. Pratt)

Local Information Centres

North West Tourist Board
The Last Drop Village
Bromley Cross, Bolton
Lancashire BL7 9PZ
(0204) 591511

Chester
Town Hall, Northgate Street
Cheshire CH1 2NF
(0244) 40144 Ext. 2111

Wales Tourist Board
Brunel House, 2 Fitzalan Road
Cardiff CF2 1UY
(0222) 499909

Mold
Town Hall, Earl Street
Gwynedd CH7 1AB
(03452) 59331

Llangollen
Town Hall, Clwyd LL20 5PD
(0978) 860828

Automobile Association
Chester Centre, 36–38 Frodsham St
Chester, Cheshire CH1 3JB
(0244) 351111

Travel

RAC road information
Stockport (061) 4776500
Rail information
Chester (0244) 40170
Bus information
Chester (0244) 47452
Air information
Manchester (061) 4893000

David & Charles produce a wide ranging list of books. The full catalogue is £1 but write to us and we will send you a copy with our compliments.

Nature Reserves

The Royal Society for Nature Conservation (0522-752326) provides contacts for local Wildlife Trusts who can advise on the best nature reserves to visit.

Touring Companions want you to enjoy the countryside without any problems for you, other visitors, or the people who must live and work there all year round. Please remember that there is no general right to wander in the countryside, although trespass is seldom a criminal offence. Stay on the rights of way marked on the Ordnance Survey map unless there is clear indication that access is permitted, or you have asked permission. Remember that not all disused railway lines are open to the public. Always obey the Country Code.

Enjoy the countryside and respect its life and work.
Guard against all risk of fire.
Fasten all gates.
Keep your dogs under close control.
Keep to public paths across farmland.
Use gates and stiles to cross fences, hedges and walls.
Leave livestock, crops and machinery alone.
Take your litter home.
Help to keep all water clean.
Protect wildlife, plants and trees.
Take special care on country roads.
Make no unnecessary noise.

National Grid references reproduced by permission of the Ordnance Survey, Southampton.

Ellesmere Port Boat Museum (Ref: 4077. Picture: D. Pratt)

Beeston Castle Viewed from the Shropshire Union Canal (Ref: 5260. Picture: D. Pratt)

Authors and artists in this volume include:

A. Burton, A. & A. Heaton, S. S. Kind, D. Young, E. Danielson, S. Qureshi, J. Slocombe, R. Laight, A. Clift, E. Dooks.